The Best of Serbia Meals

Experience the Goodness of Serbia Food

By

Heston Brown

Thank you so much for buying my book! I want to give you a special gift!

Receive a special gift as a thank you for buying my book. Now you will be able to benefit from free and discounted book offers that are sent directly to your inbox every week.

To subscribe simply fill in the box below with your details and start reaping the rewards! A new deal will arrive every day and reminders will be sent so you never miss out. Fill in the box below to subscribe and get started!

https://heston-brown.getresponsepages.com

Table of Contents

Recipe 1: Serbian Salad (Salad)

Favorite salad in Serbia – perfectly goes with every kind of meat dish.

It can be eaten alone because it is very tasty. So, this can be the perfect meal for vegetarians!

Total Prep Time: 10 minutes

Yield: 4

List of Ingredients:

- 5 tomatoes
- 3 fresh peppers
- 2 hot peppers
- 3 cucumbers
- 1 onion
- salt
- 2 tablespoons of oil

XXXXXXXXXXXXXXXXXXXXXXXXXXXXXXXXXXXXXXXXXXXXXXXXXX

Methods:

1. Wash the tomatoes and cut them into slices.

2. Peel the cucumber and cut them into rectangle pieces. Do the same with the onion.

3. Cut the pepper into slices.

4. Mix all the ingredients in one bowl. Add salt and oil.

5. Enjoy your healthy salad!

Recipe 2: "Prženice"– Fried Bread with Eggs (Breakfast)

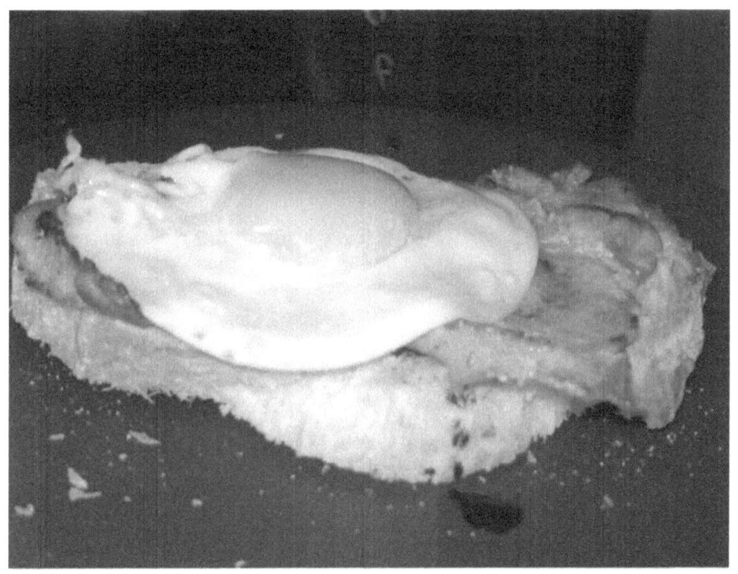

In Serbia, you do not quite throw food away. This is especially related to bread. You should always eat it (no matter what) or feed it to the poor. It is an old belief that you should NEVER throw the bread away, because if you do – you will be hungry and without anything soon.

Even today, Serbian grandmothers often may say: "Kids in Africa are hungry, and you want to throw your food in the trash bin? Eat it now!"

So, if you want to be like Serbs – not wanting to throw your food, this meal is perfect for you. Made mostly with old bread (when it becomes dry), fried eggs. Really easy to make, absolutely affordable, useful, and most of all- tasty!

Total Prep Time: 15 Minutes

Yield: 2

List of Ingredients:

- 4 slices of bread
- 2 eggs
- Pinch of salt
- ½ cup of oil
- Half glass of water

XXXXXXXXXXXXXXXXXXXXXXXXXXXXXXXXXXXXXXXXXXXXXXXXXXXXX

Methods:

1. Put the eggs in the bowl, add water and salt. Mix it with the egg-beater.

2. Soak the slices of bread in the mixture.

3. Heat the oil in the frying pan.

4. Put the slices in the pan to fry.

5. Fry for about 5 minutes on each side.

6. You can eat it with cheese, milk or yogurt.

Recipe 3: "Proja" – Corn Pie With Cheese (Breakfast)

Every Serbian old lady will tell you that the breakfast is the most important meal of the day. You have got to start with strong food so that you have concentration and strength for a long day that comes. Serbian version of corn pie is called "proja" or "projara", and it is very common in Serbia. It is believed that a Serbian hero called "Nikac from Rovine" had eaten this every morning and that he could run faster than the deer.

Total Prep Time: 30 Minutes

Yield: 4

List of Ingredients:

- 12 tablespoons of corn flour
- 3 eggs
- 1 cup of yogurt
- 1 cup of mineral water
- 10 oz. of white cheese
- Baking powder

XXXXXXXXXXXXXXXXXXXXXXXXXXXXXXXXXXXXXXXXXXXXXXXXXXXX

Methods:

1. Chop the cheese into small pieces. (Size to taste)

2. Pour just a little oil in the cupcake mold. If you do not have a cupcake mold you can use just a regular baking dish.

3. Mix all the ingredients in one big plate (container) with the small pieces of cheese.

4. Fill the cupcake molds (baking dish) with the resulting mixture.

5. Bake at 375°F for 30 minutes.

6. Serve it with yogurt and enjoy!

Recipe 4: "Popara" – Bread In Cheese (Breakfast)

Another way to eat your old bread and prevent your grandmother from complaining about your bad habits. This meal is also made with old bread. This time – with cheese.

It is not as often eaten as "prženice", but it is far from rare on the Serbian tables.

Total Prep Time: 15 Minutes

Yield: 3 to 4

List of Ingredients:

- Old bread
- 1 cube of butter
- 18 oz. of cream cheese
- ½ cup of water
- ½ cup of milk
- Pinch of salt

Methods:

1. Cut the bread into square pieces.

2. Pour water in a pan. Add salt and the diced butter.

3. When the water boils, reduce the heat, add the milk and the bread.

4. Stir gently with wooden spoon, and let it boil.

5. Add the cheese and cream.

6. Cook for a few minutes.

7. Beware not to eat it too hot!

Recipe 5: "Burek" – Pie With Meat (Breakfast)

"Burek" is mainly food of Serbian Muslims. Food for which ancestry is not yet completely defined. It is believed that "burek" came in Balkan from old Turks, who wanted to conquer Europe in the 14th century. The Turks brought us trouble and slavery, but there is a single positive thing – they bring their food with them.

One study showed that "burek" is the most often eaten meal for breakfast in Serbia (probably in the whole region of Ex-Yugoslavia) because its fat gives us the strength for work that follows. It is not very expensive, in Serbian bakeries its price usually does not exceed over $1.50. There are even bakeries that make ONLY "burek". Those ones are called – "buregdzinice".

It must be eaten with yogurt because it will take all its fat, of which burek has a lot.

Total Prep Time: 35-40 Minutes

Yield: 4

List of Ingredients:

- 1 pound of minced meat (any kind)
- Pack of cream
- Egg
- ½ baking powder
- Half glass of water
- Pinch of salt
- 5 layers of phyllo dough

xxxxxxxxxxxxxxxxxxxxxxxxxxxxxxxxxxxxxxxxxxxxxxxxxxxx

Methods:

1. Pour oil in a pan and stew the onions.

2. Put the meat in a pan and fry until you feel it is over. Add the spice to taste.

3. With egg-beater stir the cream, water and egg. Add a little salt and a baking powder.

4. Pour oil in a baking dish (where burek will bake). At the bottom of the baking tray, place 3 layers of dough. Then arrange a little bit of minced meat and sprinkle with 3-4 tablespoons of sauce. (obtained from step No3)

5. Then, put 2 layers more and repeat the procedure. Repeat until you are out of the ingredients.

6. Bake at 375°F for 35 to 40 minutes.

7. Enjoy it with yogurt.

Recipe 6: Chicken Liver with Eggs (Breakfast)

One more meal with undefined origin. There is a lot of countries that make this meal, but as far as I know, there is nowhere the same as on Balkan.

This meal has extremely high levels of proteins. Eggs and liver today are the favourite food of Serbian bodybuilders. In traditional Serbia, this meal was eaten by the people who played an old sport called "kamena s' ramena", which literally means "throwing rocks from shoulder".

This sport is based on the competition of throwing a stone into the distance. There was no prize, but the Serbian women were watching. So, you now know why this meal was essential!

It may not look attractive on the first sight, but we can assure you that it is delicious! Chicken liver is very cheap, and you can buy it in every butcher shop or market. Also, it is very easy to make.

Total Prep Time: 20 Minutes

Yield: 4

List of Ingredients:

- 18 oz. of chicken liver

- 6 eggs

- 1 onion (optional)

- 1/3 cup of oil

- spices: pepper, salt

xxxxxxxxxxxxxxxxxxxxxxxxxxxxxxxxxxxxxxxxxxxxxxxxxxxxx

Methods:

1. Wash and clean the liver. Keep only good pieces.

2. Let the frying pan heat and add the oil.

3. Put the onion in a frying pan and let it fry for a few minutes. If you do not like onion, skip this step.

4. Add the oil and the liver into the pan.

5. Add spices and let it fry for about 15 minutes.

6. You can serve it with yogurt or even potato. Enjoy!

Recipe 7: "Zapečene Tikvice" – Baked Zucchini (Breakfast)

This vegetable is very common in the Serbian kitchen, mostly because it is cheap and very very tasty – if baked right. It is used in various meals. "Tikvice" can be used as a side dish meal, but they are often used for the main course.

Total Prep Time: 35-40 Minutes

Yield: 4

List of Ingredients:

- Small zucchini
- 1.5 oz. of butter
- 3.5 oz. of cream
- 3 eggs
- Spices: pepper, salt
- Clove of garlic

Methods:

1. Peel the zucchini and cut it into small circles

2. Grind the butter with fork, add eggs, cream, garlic and mix it all together.

3. Put the zucchini in the baking dish and pour the resulting mixture on it. Add spices to taste.

4. Bake at 400°F for 25 to 30 minutes.

Recipe 8: Eggs with Spinach (Breakfast)

Another really nice meal that is perfect for Sunday family breakfast.

Maybe you did not know how perfect this combination is. It may not seem like that to you, but if it is prepared well – it can be a really tasty meal.

Very easy to make, and will definitely keep your stomach full-fed until lunch.

Total Prep Time: 15 minutes

Yield: 4

List of Ingredients:

- 8 eggs
- 6 tablespoons of milk
- 18 oz. of spinach
- 1 onion
- 1/3 glass of oil
- Salt and pepper

XXXXXXXXXXXXXXXXXXXXXXXXXXXXXXXXXXXXXXXXXXXXXXXXXXX

Methods:

1. Wash and clean the spinach. Put the spinach into the boiling water and let it cook for a few minutes. After that, strain the water.

2. Cut the onion into small pieces and put them in the frying pan. Add spinach milk. Fry for 5 minutes with constant mixing. Add salt and paper to taste.

3. In a different frying pan, prepare poached eggs.

4. Serve it together. Bon appetit!

Recipe 9: "Gibanica" – Pie With Cheese (Breakfast)

Often used as a side dish in Serbia, but people eat it at any possible time, because it tastes amazingly good. It is believed that "gibanica" is the first meal that a mother in law teaches her son's new wife when she comes to live with them. (In traditional Serbia, couples were always living with the husband parents)

It is a very sacred and respected meal in Serbia. Even today, this dish is worn on the grave of the decedent on Orthodox day of the dead called "Zadušnice". Traditional Serbs eat this meal almost every day.

Total Prep Time: 35-40 Minutes

Yield: 5

List of Ingredients:

- 1 package of phyllo dough
- 18 oz. of cheese
- 4 eggs
- 1/3 cup of mineral water
- 1/3 cup of oil
- 1 tablespoon salt

XXXXXXXXXXXXXXXXXXXXXXXXXXXXXXXXXXXXXXXXXXXXXXXXXXXX

Methods:

1. With egg-beater mix the eggs, salt, mineral water, and oil together.

2. Add cheese in the mixture.

3. Mix until you are left with small pieces of cheese. If the mixture is too thick you can add small amount of milk or yogurt.

4. Put three layers of pie crust on the bottom of your baking dish. Cover the crust with mixture, and then pile the crust one by one.

5. Coat each layer equally until you are all out of mixture and crust.

Recipe 10: Soup with Chicken Meat and Vegetables (Soup)

Not a single Sunday in Serbia could not pass without this tasty meal. This meal is marked with the beautiful smell of cooked meat, melted meat-flavoured vegetables, and noodles.

Every Serbian grandma mastered this meal in her own way, and when you get used to your grandma's soup – it will forever be the best one for you. This can be a problem – young wives in Serbia are very frustrated with making soup because they could never make them as good as grandmothers.

Some families eat this kind of soup, literally, every day – and there is nothing strange with that.

Total Prep Time: 140 minutes

Yield: 4

List of Ingredients:

- 10 oz. of chicken meat
- 1 carrot
- 1-2 potatoes
- 1 onion
- 1 celery
- 1 parsley
- 1 pack of noodles
- Salt and pepper to taste
- 8 cups of water

XXXXXXXXXXXXXXXXXXXXXXXXXXXXXXXXXXXXXXXXXXXXXXXXXXXX

Methods:

1. Wash and cut the vegetables into the small pieces.

2. Put them in one big bowl, and fill it with water.

3. Add meat in any form you like. You can either cut it into small or regular pieces.

4. Add salt, pepper, and parsley.

5. Cook for 120 minutes. After that, add the noodles and cook for 10 minutes more.

Recipe 11: Veal Soup with Vegetables (Soup)

Second favorite soup in Serbia, because Serbs are cultivating chickens and pigs much more than other animals. It is often eaten in a restaurant, rather than home – because it is a little bit harder to make, but I am sure that you will make it well!

It is not eaten as often as chicken soup, but it can be even tastier.

Total Prep Time: 200 minutes

Yield: 6

List of Ingredients:

- 1 onion
- 3 tablespoons of oil
- 2 carrots
- 2 potatoes
- 2 tablespoons of flour
- 2 yolks
- ½ glasses of cream
- Fresh parsley
- 9 cups of water
- 1 lemon

XXXXXXXXXXXXXXXXXXXXXXXXXXXXXXXXXXXXXXXXXXXXXXXXXXXXX

Methods:

1. Cut the onion into small pieces.

2. Pour the oil into a bowl and heat it up. Add the onion and let it fry for a few minutes.

3. Cut the meat into rectangular pieces and add it to the bowl. Add 8 cups of water. Also, cut the lemon and add it.

4. Clean the carrot and potatoes, then cut them. Add it to the mixture along with the spices. Let it cook.

5. In a different bowl, mix the flour with a cup of water. Add resulting mixture to the bowl with meat and vegetables. Cook until water boils.

6. With egg beater, mix the yolks with cream.

7. After 180 minutes, remove the boiled soup from the burner. Add only 1 or 2 kitchen spoons of soup with the yolk-cream mixture. Mix it for a while, and then pour everything in the same bowl.

Recipe 12: Serbian Pizza (Lunch)

Another Italian meal in Serbian kitchen!

These two cultures have not mixed in terms of religion and language so much, but they have a certain common point – and one of the best is food.

It is believed that the first real pizza was made by the poor, so it is very affordable to make.

So, cheap, that Serbs up to 20 years ago could not believe that you can buy a single pizza cut – because it was so cheap to make. In Serbia, you could not really buy it that way.

Total Prep Time: 40 minutes

Yield: 5

List of Ingredients:

- For dough:
- 3 tablespoons of flour
- ½ pack of yeast
- ½ cup of beer
- ½ tablespoons of sugar
- 1 tablespoon of oil
- 1 tablespoon of salt

For topping:

- 3 tomatoes (or tomato juice)

- 8 oz. of cheese

- 8 oz. of sausage

- 4 oz. of bacon

- 1 egg

- Oregano

- Pepper

XXXXXXXXXXXXXXXXXXXXXXXXXXXXXXXXXXXXXXXXXXXXXXXXXXXX

Methods:

Making dough

1. Mix all the ingredients (for making the dough). And then stir it by hands. Add beer at the end. The dough should be medium soft.

2. Pour the oil into the bottom of casserole dish and put the dough in. Cover the casserole dish with a cloth and leave it aside while preparing ingredients for filling.

Making topping:

1. Cut the sausage, bacon, and tomato.

2. With egg beater – mix the egg with cheese.

3. Now, it is time to put the topping on the dough. We put ingredients in this order: tomato, cheese, and egg, sausage, bacon.

4. Bake for 30 minutes at 400°F.

5. Enjoy this delicious Serbian pizza with pepperoni or hot peppers!

Recipe 13: "Karadjordjeva Šnicla"
– Pork Steak (Lunch)

Karadjordje was a founder of modern Serbia. He was chosen as the leader of the First Serbian Uprising in 1804. The First Serbian Uprising was an uprising of Serbs against the Ottoman Empire, after more than 400 years of slavery.

Serbs choose Karadjordje as their leader because he was very strict, strong and respected among the people. After the uprising, he became Serbian's Prince and its monarchy is still the first in Serbia. His cousin, Alexander Karadjordjevic is the current Prince.

Karadjordje's steak is a Serbian breaded cutlet dish. It is first made by Serbian chef – Mica Stojanovic for some cooking competition. God knows why he called this dish this way, but he earned The Order of Karađorđe's Star for it. In Serbia – it is a great honor.

This dish is often eaten in Serbian restaurants, and people often call it "Devojacki san" or "Woman's dream". Do not ask why – just look at the picture.

Total Prep Time: 40-45 Minutes

Yield: 5-6

List of Ingredients:

- 35 oz. pork steaks

- 6 thicker sheets of bacon

- 10 oz. of cream cheese

- 5 oz. of regular cheese

- Pepper and salt

For frying:

- Breadcrumbs

- Flour

- 3 Eggs

- A lot of oil

XXXXXXXXXXXXXXXXXXXXXXXXXXXXXXXXXXXXXXXXXXXXXXXXXXXX

Methods:

1. Flatten the steaks with the hammer for meat. Rub the spices on the steak, and let it sit for a few minutes.

2. Chop the bacon into little rectanglare pieces. Grate the regular cheese, and mix it together.

3. Stretch the steak, and spread the cream cheese on it. Put the mixture of bacon and cheese on the steak and roll it like in the picture:

4. First, soak the rolled steak in a plate with flour. Then, in a plate with egg, and finally in the breadcrumbs. (see the picture above)

5. Put the oil in the frying pan and heat it up. Add the steaks to it.

6. Fry by taste. Make sure they do not burn, by rotating the steaks from time to time.

7. When it is ready, you can add some mayonnaise on the top. Enjoy, you deserve it!

Recipe 14: Baked Pasta with Cheese and Champignons (Lunch)

Food from Italian origins, which Serbs changed in their own way.

They have made pasta from ingredients that are available to them and easily accessible. So, this is some kind of Serbian pasta.

Total Prep Time: 30 minutes

Yield: 4

List of Ingredients:

- 18 oz. of pasta (macaroni)
- 14 oz. of champignons
- 1 cup of cream
- 1 cup of yogurt
- 5 eggs
- 2 onions
- Oregano and salt to taste

XXXXXXXXXXXXXXXXXXXXXXXXXXXXXXXXXXXXXXXXXXXXXXXXXX

Methods:

1. Cut champignons along with the onions. Fry them together for a few minutes and add salt.

2. Mix all ingredients together and pour it in the casserole dish.

3. Bake for 20 minutes at 400°F. If you like them to be more baked, leave them longer.

Recipe 15: "Đuveč"– Cooked Vegetables (Pepper) (Lunch)

People who live in South Serbia are often called "paprikari" or "pepper people". The Serbian south is known for its production of pepper. So, they eat it very often.

However, this food is also usually in the Serbian North – where people do not eat pepper very often. So, this is not spicy food (like they eat on the south) – this meal is cooked pepper with some other vegetables (tomato, eggplant, onion, rice).

Total Prep Time: 40 minutes

Yield: 4

List of Ingredients:

- 4 tomatoes
- 2 red bell peppers
- 1 eggplant
- 1 onion
- 15 oz. of rice
- Salt
- 1/3 glass of oil
- ½ glass of water

XXXXXXXXXXXXXXXXXXXXXXXXXXXXXXXXXXXXXXXXXXXXXXXXXXX

Methods:

1. Put oil in the pot. Add cut onion and stew for 5 minutes.

2. Cut peppers and mix it with the onion. Add salt and continue to stew.

3. Peel the eggplant and tomato. Cut them into the small rectangular pieces. Add them in the pot along with the water.

4. Add a pinch of salt.

5. Wash the rice and also add it to the mixture.

6. Stir it from time to time – Be careful that the rice does not stick to the bottom.

7. Cook for about 20 minutes, and then let it sit for another 10 minutes.

8. You can eat it with any meat, or without anything. It is delicious in both ways!

Recipe 16: Serbian Army Bean (Lunch)

Legendary Serbian army food – because every Serbian male who was in the army (JNA) is deeply in love with this meal.

In the Serbian army – you eat beans almost every single day, and everyone will confirm that the bean is prepared in the best way there.

This recipe was kept as a secret, but after the last Balkan wars it was released in public.

Serbian army successfully won many wars in the past. They beat Ottoman Empire, Battle with Bulgarians, First and also the Second World War. Is the secret in the beans?

Total Prep Time: 190 minutes

Yield: 6

List of Ingredients:

- 30oz of beans
- 2 carrots
- 1 garlic
- 2 tablespoons of flour
- 20 oz. of pork ribs
- 20 oz. of bacon
- Half glass of oil

xxxxxxxxxxxxxxxxxxxxxxxxxxxxxxxxxxxxxxxxxxxxxxxxxxx

Methods:

1. Put the beans in the cold water and let it sit for around 120 minutes.

After that, remove the water.

2. Put the beans in the cooking pot, pour the water again and cook it for 15 minutes. Add the garlic and carrots, let it cook again. Add oil too.

3. Wash the ribs and put it in a different cooking pot. Pour the water and let it cook until it softens.

4. Add ribs and cut bacon to the beans. Cook it for another 40 minutes.

5. After that, put some oil in the frying pan. Add flour and pepper and fry for a few minutes.

6. Add this mixture in the cooking pot. Cook for another 5 minutes. Enjoy!

Recipe 17: "Musaka"– Minced Meat With Potatoes (Lunch)

Not quite a Serbian meal, but it is very common in modern Serbia. It is believed that this dish was originally from Greece, and through them, it came to Serbia.

This meal can easily become vegetarian – just replace the meat with the eggplants.

Total Prep Time: 60 minutes

Yield: 5

List of Ingredients:

54 | P a g e

- 35 oz. of potato
- 18 oz. minced meat
- ½ onion
- 1 tablespoon of small pepper
- 2 tablespoons of salt
- 8 tablespoons of water
- 6 tablespoons of olive oil
- 4 eggs
- 1 cup of milk
- 1 tablespoon of flour

XXXXXXXXXXXXXXXXXXXXXXXXXXXXXXXXXXXXXXXXXXXXXXXXXXXX

Methods:

1. Peel the potato. Cut it into slices and put them in the bowl. Add 2 tablespoons of oil, 1 tablespoon of salt and mix it all together.

2. In a different bowl, mix minced meat with 1 tablespoon of pepper, 1 tablespoon of salt and cut onions. Stir it, and then add 4 tablespoons of oil and 8 tablespoon of water.

3. Third bowl – mix eggs, milk, and flour. Mix it with mixer.

4. Pour the rest of the oil on the bottom of the baking dish.

5. Put a row of potatoes on the bottom. Put a row of meat over it and then again, a row of potatoes and so on. There should be 5 layers (3 of potatoes and 2 of meat).

6. Pour the mixture with eggs and milk on top of everything.

7. Bake for 40 minutes at 375° F.

Recipe 18: "Pihtije"– Meat In Gelatin (Lunch)

Another Serbian meal in series: "I could not believe this is actually delicious".

Modern Serbia is divided into 2 sides. Those who love this meal, and those who have never tried it.

Those who adore "pihtije", organize various manifestations and competitions in making them. So, it is a very popular, and unique Serbian meal.

Total Prep Time: Around 140 minutes + waiting

Yield: 5

List of Ingredients:

- 4 pig legs (fresh or smoked)

- 1 pork knee

- 1 bay leaf

- 6-7 pieces of garlic

- 1 parsley

- 6-7 large onions garlic

- Salt to taste

XXXXXXXXXXXXXXXXXXXXXXXXXXXXXXXXXXXXXXXXXXXXXXXXXX

Methods:

1. Wash pork legs and knee. Put them in the cooking pot. Add the bay leaf and spices to taste. Fill the pot with water.

2. Cook for 120 minutes, or until it softens.

3. Pour the liquid from cooking pot in some other bowl and let it cook again.

4. Separate the meat from the bones and put the meat on the bottom of a casserole dish.

5. When liquid is boiled – add the cut onions, garlic, parsley and salt. Mix it and pour it on the meat.

6. Put "pihtije" in the fridge and let it sit the whole night. The next day, remove the fat from the top of the pihtije.

7. Cut it into rectangular pieces. If you think you have done well, come to Serbian city Rumenka, so you can participate in the competition!

Recipe 19: "Ražnjić" – Meat On The Stick (Lunch)

There are certain cities in Serbia, which are special for preparing this barbecue meal.

Leskovac is one of the best destinations for food tourism – because they are the world champions in barbecue. Their recipes and traditions are a strictly guarded secret.

However, every Serb claim to know the best way to prepare this specialty, so I will describe it, in the way we prepare it in our home (backyard).

Meat should always be prepared on the grill (not on the fire, like the people from the USA do).

Total Prep Time: 30 minutes

Yield: 5

List of Ingredients:

- 18 oz. of chicken/pork meat

- 2-3 tomatoes

- 3 onions

- 14 oz. of champignons

- Few slices of bacon

xxxxxxxxxxxxxxxxxxxxxxxxxxxxxxxxxxxxxxxxxxxxxxxxxxxxxxxx

Methods:

1. Cut the onions into small pieces and put it in the bottom of your container (where you will later put prepared meat).

2. Wash and cut the meat into small rectangular pieces.

3. Wash the tomatoes and champignons.

4. The order on a stick is not so important. We put ingredients on the stick in this order:

1 champignon – piece of meat – piece of tomato – piece of meat – 1 champignon

5. With the given ingredients, you should make 5 or 6

6. When you arrange the stick, put it on the grill and cook for a few minutes. Be careful not to burn it, turn it regularly. It would be good to pour some beer on the grilled stick.

7. When it is done, put it in the container with onions, and mix. It would be better If you could close the lid of the container and mix it like that.

Recipe 20: "Škembići"- (Lunch)

Favorite food of ex-Yugoslavian socialist. It is considered as a delicacy to laborers. Now, it is usually eaten in "kafana" (Serbian taverns).

At first, people do not want to try this at all. But, after they try – they ask for more!

It is a kind of soup with pork offals (stomach). So, it is very cheap to make – but do not worry, it is delicious too!!

Total Prep Time: 240 minutes

Yield: 6

List of Ingredients:

- 35 oz. of pork offals
- 2 onions
- 2 garlic cloves
- Half glass of oil
- 2 tablespoons of flour
- Pepper and salt

XXXXXXXXXXXXXXXXXXXXXXXXXXXXXXXXXXXXXXXXXXXXXXXXXXX

Methods:

1. Wash and cut pork offals into small pieces. Put it in the bowl along with the water and cook for 3 hours. Change the water every hour, so you can be sure that you have removed all the unpleasant smells.

2. Cut onions and garlic and put them in the frying pan along with the oil. Add flour and spices. Fry just for a few minutes and then add it to the bowl with offals.

3. Cook for another 60 minutes. You can serve it with cheese!

Recipe 21: "Sarma"– Stuffed Cabbage (Lunch)

Definitely, one of the favourite meal in Serbia.

Orthodox Serbs are the only people who are celebrating "The Slava" – day in a year when you show respect to your saint. On that glory day – the main food on the table is, of course, SARMA.

Total Prep Time: 250 minutes

Yield: 5

List of Ingredients:

- 35 oz. of ground pork

- 1 glass of rice

- 2 pieces of medium-sized onions

- A small piece of garlic

- 5 oz. of bacon

- ½ tablespoons of hot pepper

- 1 slice of sweet milled peppers

- 2 cabbage heads

XXXXXXXXXXXXXXXXXXXXXXXXXXXXXXXXXXXXXXXXXXXXXXXXXX

Methods:

1. Cut the onions and garlic into small rectangular pieces. Stew for a few minutes.

2. Add small pieces of bacon to the frying pan (with onions and garlic).

3. Wash the rice and add it in the frying pan too.

4. Then, add the meat, along with the spices.

5. Make meatballs from this mixture.

6. In a pot, cook the cabbage just for a couple of minutes –
to soften. Separate the cabbage layers and cut the thick
parts.

7. Take one cabbage layer on your hand, and then put the
meatball on it. (Look at picture)

8. Roll it like a paper. Side by side.

9. Put the given cabbage rolls in some large bowl. Fill it
with water and you can add a bay leaf and tomato juice by
taste.

10. Cook it for 4 hours at 375° F.

Recipe 22: "Uštipak"(Diner)

Another meal originated from Bosnian Serbs, but now, it is being eaten in every side of the Balkan.

Total Prep Time: 15 – 20 minutes

Yield: 5

List of Ingredients:

- 10 oz. of flour
- 2 cups of milk
- 2 eggs
- Pinch of salt
- ½ glass of oil

XXXXXXXXXXXXXXXXXXXXXXXXXXXXXXXXXXXXXXXXXXXXXXX

Methods:

1. Mix the flour, eggs, milk and salt with mixer.

2. Heat the oil in the frying pan.

3. With tablespoon, add the mixture in the frying pan.

4. When the corner of Ustipak becomes golden, rotate it and fry the other side. It should not be longer than just 20-30 seconds.

5. Remove the Ustipak from the frying pan and put them on the plate with paper. (To collect the fat)

6. Eat it with the cheese, cream or chocolate. Yes, it could be dessert too!

Recipe 23: "Police"– Potato, Cheese And Bacon (Diner)

Traditional food from Bosnian Serbs.

In the past, they have prepared this meal outside, under the fire – but in modern days, we prepare it in the oven.

This meal is from the region called Lika, where the strongest Serbs have lived. It is believed that they could kill a bear with bare hands.

Total Prep Time: 60 minutes

Yield: 6

List of Ingredients:

- 8 potatoes
- A little bit of butter
- 6 oz. of thick bacon
- 3.5 oz. of cheese
- Salt

xxxxxxxxxxxxxxxxxxxxxxxxxxxxxxxxxxxxxxxxxxxxxxxxxxxxxxxx

Methods:

1. Peel and cut the potatoes in half.

2. Put a little bit of butter on each half. Add salt.

3. Put it in the oven and bake for 40 – 45 minutes. (375°F)

4. After that, add 1 slice of bacon on each half and bake again for 10 minutes more.

5. When it is done, remove it from the oven and add some cheese to melt on the potatoes.

6. Serve it with the yogurt and some salad. (Tomato or cucumbers)

Recipe 24: "Umak"– Eggs With Cheese (Diner)

Very easy to make. This meal can be eaten for breakfast too.

Total Prep Time: 10 minutes

Yield: 4

List of Ingredients:

- 8 eggs

- 12-18 oz. of cheese (feta)

- salt to taste

- ½ glass of oil

XXXXXXXXXXXXXXXXXXXXXXXXXXXXXXXXXXXXXXXXXXXXXXXXXXX

Methods:

1. Mix the eggs with egg-beater. Add salt.

2. Pour the oil in the frying pan to heat. After a few minutes, add the eggs.

3. Fry it for 2 minutes and then add small parts of cheese. Mix it together

4. Fry for 6 or 7 minutes. (To taste)

Recipe 25: Homemade Pie with Cherries (Dessert)

In June, almost every village in Serbia is colored red because of this beautiful fruit. Everyone has at least one cherry tree.

So, Serbs come up with this delicious pie, so that they would not have to throw these cherries away. The best is from ripe cherries because they are sweet.

Total Prep Time: 40 minutes

Yield: 5

List of Ingredients:

- 21 oz. of cherries
- 10 tablespoons of sugar
- 9 tablespoon of pudding (vanilla)
- 18 oz. of thick pie crust
- ½ glass of water
- 1/3 glass of oil

XXXXXXXXXXXXXXXXXXXXXXXXXXXXXXXXXXXXXXXXXXXXXXXXXXXX

Methods:

1. Make pudding with vanilla flavor.

2. Clean cherries (remove the cherry stone).

3. Mix the cherries with pudding. Add 10 tablespoon of sugar.

4. Pile up the 3 layers of crust in the casserole dish. Pour the mix of oil and water on each one, along with the sugar.

5. Add 3 layers more with cherry/pudding fill.

6. Roll it into a cylinder shape.

7. Bake at 375°F for 30 minutes. When it is done – pour powdered sugar on the pie by taste.

Recipe 26: "Baklava"(Dessert)

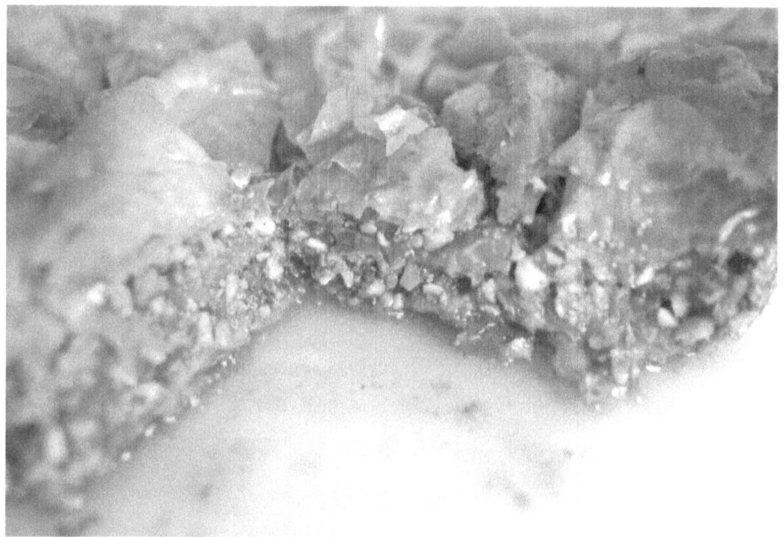

This is another rare good thing that Turks brought with them on their Europe journey in the 14th century. They are masters of sweet products even today. The best bakeries in Serbia are run by Muslims, and by that, they are famous on the Balkan.

This oriental dessert is just perfect with the morning coffee or tea.

Total Prep Time: 120 minutes

Yield: 6

List of Ingredients:

- 18 oz. of phyllo dough

- 18 oz. of nuts – milled

- 1 glass of oil

- 5 oz. of butter

- 3 glasses of water

- 28 oz. of sugar

- 1 lemon (juice)

XXXXXXXXXXXXXXXXXXXXXXXXXXXXXXXXXXXXXXXXXXXXXXXXXXXXX

Methods:

1. First, cook sugar in the water for about 20 minutes. After that, add lemon juice. Let it cool.

2. Pour the oil in the bottom of the casserole dish. First, put the 3 layers of dough on the bottom. (Each oiled)

3. Pour the nuts on the 4th layer (3 to 4 tablespoons). 5th – just with oil.

4. Follow this order – 1 layer with nuts and then 1 with only oil until you are out of ingredients. Note that in the end, there should be 3 crusts with only oil.

5. Cut the Baklava in rectangular pieces.

6. Mix a little bit of oil with butter and pour it on the Baklava.

7. Bake for 50 minutes at 375°F.

8. After that, remove the top crust (if it is burnt). Pour the mixture of sugar and lemon juice over the baklava, and enjoy!

Recipe 27: "Bundevara"– Pumpkin Pie (Dessert)

A popular dessert from Vojvodina, because Vojvodina is famous for pumpkins grown.

People from Vojvodina are often joking about pumpkins. They say in the past, they lived in giant pumpkins instead of home.

This dessert can be perfect for your Halloween party!

Total Prep Time: 60 minutes

Yield: 6

List of Ingredients:

- 1 pumpkin
- 18 oz. of thick crust
- 20 tablespoons of sugar
- 1/3 glass of oil
- 1/3 glass of water
- Powdered sugar to taste

XXXXXXXXXXXXXXXXXXXXXXXXXXXXXXXXXXXXXXXXXXXXXXXXXX

Methods:

1. Clean and chop the pumpkin in small parts. Add sugar.

2. Mix it and let it sit for 10 minutes. Turn on the oven to heat at 375°F.

3. Pour the oil on the bottom of a casserole dish.

4. Put 4 layers of crust first on the bottom, and put the oil mixed with water on them. (Each one equally)

5. On the 4th layer – put the pumpkin pieces. Add 3 layers more. (Also with pumpkin)

6. Roll it in a cylinder shape.

7. Bake at 375°F for 50 minutes. When it is done – you can pour powdered sugar on the top!

Recipe 28: "Oblande"– Serbian Wafer (Dessert)

Very old recipe, this sweet dessert is an important aspect in every young Serb's childhood.

When we were kids we used to go out and play football on the streets every single day. Our only meal during the day was this delicious wafer. The whole board is worn, uncut.

Later, it is a common cake in weddings and "slava" tables. There are many various recipes for this dessert, but we have picked the most common one:

Total Prep Time: 10 to 15 minutes

Yield: 6

List of Ingredients:

- 30 tablespoons of milk

- 14 oz. of sugar

- 9 oz. of butter

- 7 oz. of ground biscuits

- 7 oz. of milled nuts

- 1 chocolate board

- 5 layers of wafer crust

XXXXXXXXXXXXXXXXXXXXXXXXXXXXXXXXXXXXXXXXXXXXXXXXXXXX

Methods:

1. Pour milk, sugar, and butter in one bowl and let it cook.

2. When it boils, add ground biscuits, nuts, chocolate and cook for another 2 to 3 minutes.

3. After that, remove it from the heat. Pour the resulting mixture on each layer of the crust equally. Join them together. (like gluing)

4. Cut them into any shape you want and enjoy! They are perfect with cold milk!

Recipe 29: "Bakin Kolač"– Waffle (Dessert)

This is some kind of Serbian waffle. In Serbia, they call this dessert: "Bakin kolač" which literally means: "Grandmother's cake".

That name is because every grandma in Serbia bakes this cake when you come to visit her unannounced, so she needs to make something really fast. You need some waffle device!

Total Prep Time: 10 minutes

Yield: 4

List of Ingredients:

- 3 eggs
- 9 tablespoons of sugar
- 2 tablespoons of flour
- 1 pack of vanilla sugar
- 1 baking powder
- 2 glasses of milk
- 1 cup of oil
- 1 lemon (only outer skin - scraped)

XXXXXXXXXXXXXXXXXXXXXXXXXXXXXXXXXXXXXXXXXXXXXXXXXX

Methods:

1. Mix eggs, sugar, flour, baking powder. (One by one with 1 minute delay)

2. Add lemon outer skin – scraped.

3. Add milk and oil.

4. Turn on your waffle device. Pour the mixture in it with kitchen spoon.

5. You know further! Enjoy your easy prepared dessert!

Recipe 30: "Rozen Torta"(Dessert)

One of the favorite dessert cakes that can be found on the "Slava" tables. A lot of people do not really know the name of this dessert, they just say: "Bring the plate with that rose thing to me!"

Total Prep Time: 5-6 hours (with waiting)

Yield: 6

List of Ingredients:

- 18 oz. of sugar

- 10 oz. of milled nuts

- 8 oz. of butter

- 9 layers of phyllo dough or some very thick crust

For the rose top:

- 9 oz. of powdered sugar

- ½ glass of lemon juice

- 2 glasses of water

- A little bit of color for cakes

XXXXXXXXXXXXXXXXXXXXXXXXXXXXXXXXXXXXXXXXXXXXXXXXXX

Methods:

1. Put the sugar along with the water in the bowl. Let it cook for 5 minutes.

2. After that, add nuts, butter. Let butter melt.

3. Pour the resulting mixture on the layers. Use 8 layers – leave 1 for the rose top topping.

4. Let it sit for a few hours in the fridge, or even a whole day. After that – start to make your cool rose top!

5. Put all the ingredients marked as "For the rose top" in one bowl. Mix it with the spoon.

6. Pour it over the cake and let it dry! You can organize "Slava" now in your own home!

About the Author

Heston Brown is an accomplished chef and successful e-book author from Palo Alto California. After studying cooking at The New England Culinary Institute, Heston stopped briefly in Chicago where he was offered head chef at some of the city's most prestigious restaurants. Brown decide that he missed the rolling hills and sunny weather of California and moved back to his home state to open up his own catering company and give private cooking classes.

Heston lives in California with his beautiful wife of 18 years and his two daughters who also have aspirations to follow in their father's footsteps and pursue careers in the culinary arts. Brown is well known for his delicious fish and chicken dishes and teaches these recipes as well as many others to his students.

When Heston gave up his successful chef position in Chicago and moved back to California, a friend suggested he use the internet to share his recipes with the world and so he did! To date, Heston Brown has written over 1000 e-books that contain recipes, cooking tips, business strategies for catering companies and a self-help book he wrote from personal experience.

He claims his wife has been his inspiration throughout many of his endeavours and continues to be his partner in business as well as life. His greatest joy is having all three women in his life in the kitchen with him cooking their favourite meal while his favourite jazz music plays in the background.

Author's Afterthoughts

Thank you to all the readers who invested time and money into my book! I cherish every one of you and hope you took the same pleasure in reading it as I did in writing it.

Out of all of the books out there, you chose mine and for that I am truly grateful. It makes the effort worth it when I know my readers are enjoying my work from beginning to end.

Please take a few minutes to write an Amazon review so that others can benefit from your opinions and insight. Your review will help countless other readers make an informed choice

Thank you so much,

Heston Brown

www.ingramcontent.com/pod-product-compliance
Lightning Source LLC
Chambersburg PA
CBHW031322060726
47590CB00003B/1311